Trauma lives in the cellar of the soul.

The Magic of Connection

Art of Compassionate Understanding

Stephen R. Andrew

ISBN: 978-1-0882-9644-8

Stephen R. Andrew
25 Middle Street
Portland, Maine 04101
www.hetimaine.org

Author's note

We often become anxious and overwhelmed in the face of intimacy. Our "hurts" frequently come alive inside of our relationships and our hearts are clouded with historical residue. Each day, each moment, amid our fears, anxiety, and wounds, we need to make a fundamental decision to engage with life. We need to make a daily commitment to challenge ourselves, or to let go.

This book is taken from a series of lectures given from 1987 to 1997 and is a preamble to my son, Sebastian, whom I love dearly. I started caring for my fellow human beings after having grown up under the influence of a significant amount of hurt, trauma, and serious oppression. As I come to the end of my journey, it is my hope that I may leave something of value behind for others. I humbly offer these heartfelt conversations, along with my stories of surviving the dis-ease of living in a family and community under the influence of great poverty, alcoholism, domestic violence, sexual abuse, and significant alienation. Each of these factors has affected my life, and also, led me to my life's work.

Love in Action,

[signature: Stephen L. Richer]

Acknowledgements

I would love to thank dearly people who shaped
me both personally and professionally~
Melissa S., Doug M., Kelley N., Doreen A., Alice
A., Mary C., John B., Bob K., Glenn C., Oliver S.,
Jayme V., Bob J., Linda J., David P., Marie S.,
Angelina M., Elizabeth M. L., Sarah S., Gabrielle
R. T., Terri P., Michael N., Michael M., Neil M.,
Rodney M., Jill F., Bill M., Terri M., Susan C.,
Alan L., David P., Steve B. S., Stefan, Geoff K.,
Dottie F., Tom C. Stan E., Mindy, Dino, Li B.,
friends in the MINT community and all the
people in our mutual aid support groups in the
last 35 years...all of the donors to our nonprofit,
Agape Inc., InnerEdge and Dignity ...

Special thanks to Lacey S. for editing help.

Hilary, Sebastian, Jeff S. Deborah S., Coral S.,
Joan A., John P. Robin C., Susan P, Michael P.,
Blaine H., Christine M., and the Kindred Spirits
community.

*We change people
through the heart*

The Magic of
Connection

The first thing I would like to do, to start things off, is to say that my particular life is one in which I have experienced an incredible amount of trauma. I would describe my own personal background as one of those people who has had to witness, on a regular basis, violence of the soul, and somebody who has had to experience a lot of relationship conflict. Conflict, violence, and criticism on a regular basis brings to us a certain kind of injury. This trauma and oppression gets stored in our bodies, it literally gets stored in our cells, and I refer to that as a trauma whisper.

I'm a proud father, and when my son was a toddler, I noticed that he didn't have a lot of fear. What he would do would be to go about his life in a way that challenged it. He would bang into something, fall to the floor, and cry. Because when he would get hurt, he noticed it and he discharged the hurt. Then he would go about doing other things, but he held that hurt as a memory.

I'm reminded of this wonderful story about this young boy named Michael. Michael lived in a healthy family, I understand there are four of them and they have all gotten invitations to the Smithsonian Institute. So, if you didn't get an invitation, you're not in one of those families. But Michael grew up in a healthy family. One day, when he was about seven, he closed the car door and he caught his finger in the door. When he caught his finger in the door, the pain rushed up his hand and went right into his mind, and his brain said, "OUCH!" Then, he started to cry and he started to let out the tears like "Aaah!" because it rushes right through the entire system. It's like a circle: the hurt happens, the pain goes into our brain, it signals, "Let out the energy" and as the energy goes out, believe it or not, there is another part that happens. The injury starts to heal. All part of a circle, the circle of life. We get injured, we feel the feeling, we feel it in its fullness, and then when we do that, the healing begins.

So Michael is caught in the pain but,

of course, he's a boy and he's learned that what you do when you're in pain is that you take your other hand, which is not injured, and you stick your hand in your eye, trying to stop the leakage. Do you notice what else we do? We take all of the tears and we pull them back inside. We do all of this just to make sure we stop leaking what is our true emotion about hurt. What he's doing is pulling it back in. But, he grew up in a healthy family. He walks into the kitchen, and his mother takes him into the bathroom and nurses his wound. At the same time, she notices that he's not speaking about it, so she says to him, "Michael, what happened?" Well, the minute she asked, it came roaring back up. I don't know if you've ever felt this happen, but when somebody brings it up it always comes came roaring back. "I got caught in the car door!" And he's letting out this kind of energy again, but he's learning how to pull it back in. He was in a healthy family, the other caregiver, the other parent, came in and noticed his bandage and said, "Tell me what happened." Michael repeated, "I got caught in the car door." with less intensity than the last time he told the story. Then his brother, I said this was a very healthy family, asked him, "Tell me what happened Michael." "Oh, my hand got caught in the car door." You see, your memory doesn't change. You remember the event, but the feeling of the event and its intensity is gone.

What you need to see in the story of Michael is that you have to tell the story as many times as you can and keep attached to the emotional parts of it until it moves through your body so that you can allow the vacuum, the hole, the space to open up again. You'll hear it in people's stories. It happened to me today where this wonderful woman is sitting across from me, and she's looking at me, and she says, "My relationships have been so awful, what I'm going to do is never be in another one." What she's talking about is the psychic pain, the energy of the hurt has been so bad that she just doesn't want to go there anymore. But I just want to tell you a secret, and that is she still yearns for a mutually empowering intimate relationship. Now, what has developed is the hurt, the anger, the conflict has developed this fear. The real reason that she doesn't want to go there is because, "I don't want to feel that feeling again." If you take it even a step further, it's, "I'm afraid to have that happen to me again."

You see, I tell you about the healthy family of Michael, but what I really want to do is tell you about the other story. You see Michael got his hand caught in the car door. That's true. And he cried, and he pulled it in, and he walked into the kitchen. And when he walked into the kitchen, his mother turned to him and said, "Can't you do anything right? Get into the bathroom and take care of it." He had all of this pain and hurt, and I don't know if you can imagine what a seven-year-old would do with an injured hand, but you know how he took care of it. Right? He really took care of it. He wrapped the pain all around his body and then he came out to the kitchen. And I don't know if you've ever felt it, but that hurt sits right there, like a softball, when all you want to do is connect with another human being. So, he's bouncing around the kitchen hoping, hoping that maybe he'll connect to his mother, and that maybe he'll be able to tell the story in a way that's not shaming. He's sitting there in the kitchen and she says, "Can't you do anything right?" He goes back into the bathroom and he snips away, and this time he hides his hand in his jacket. That's not really the worst part of the story. He walks through the kitchen, he tiptoes now, because he's afraid. Of what? He is afraid of shame. He doesn't want to be criticized again, so he goes outside. But that's not the part of the story I really want to tell you about, even though that's painful enough.

At about age thirty-two, Michael was in the car with his godson, who happened to be little Scotty who was about seven-years old. Little Scotty, slammed the car door and all of a sudden Michael started to scream at Scotty. He went, "Scotty be careful!" He didn't understand where all of that energy came from. And I don't know if you can imagine what Scotty must have felt like. Little Scotty was ducking down. "What did I do?" He hadn't injured himself, all he did was slam the car door.

Every one of the places we've been hurt in our lives are stored in our bodies, and when something familiar happens, that looks just like it feels like it, sounds like it, smells like it, it brings it all right back up, all of the fear. It brings it all back up. You see, I was Michael. I screamed at Scotty that day, and I had to remember that when I was a small boy, at the age of seven, I had gotten my finger caught in the car door, and I remember that my mother was very shaming and very angry about the way I was clumsy. I didn't really tell anybody about it until I told this little boy. I said, "I'm sorry, Scotty. I'm sorry. I didn't mean to yell at you, but when I was a small boy, I got injured by the car door." You see, it's stored in our bodies, and when it gets stored, it creates fear.

There are three things that we are afraid of because they happen to us, and once they happen to you, they are stored in your body. The best thing that you can do is be with other people where you can tell your story over and over and explore the different ways it impacts your life.

Fear number one is abandonment. We are afraid to lean toward people, to welcome them, to reach out to them, and to call them up when we are thinking about them because we are afraid they will be mad or abandon us or push us away. It does happen. You have lots of reasons to believe that. But the issue isn't whether it happens or doesn't happen, you can't prevent it. But you see the more times you've been abandoned, the more you start to put a scanner on your head. You literally put a scanner on your head and you start looking at the world through the eyes of abandonment. What you do is you watch for it, and since you watch for it, you can find it everywhere. You can find it in anybody's story. You gather with a group of people and you're now looking for abandonment. You're looking forward to seeing someone you had a really good connection with last week. You come walking in, and they're talking to somebody else and they don't even say "Hi" to you. You're now thinking, "What did I do? What is it about me?" It's not about you at all, but the fear starts. It sets off a recording, and the only reason that it's there is because it's an echo of the past, the trauma whisper.

FEAR – False Evidence Appearing Real. It's false, but feels and appears real. Ninety-seven percent of all fear is false, and it all *feels* real. We're riddled with fear, and we only have two choices. It breaks down to these two choices no matter how complex it is. You can either love, or you can be in fear. That's it. That's the only two choices you have. People can either love you fully, or you can be in fear, or they can be in fear, that's it. They may be angry, but that is a secondary emotion to fear. You can be in shame and say, "I can't do this." But that is only fear.

Some of you might say, "I need to exercise." And you say that to yourself monthly, weekly, some of you even have ten or twelve gym memberships over the last few years. You've joined a gym and gotten a trainer and you go for a while and then you stop going. Anybody ever had that happen to them besides me? Just two or three of us, okay, the rest of us have got it all together. I'm glad I'm talking to this audience and maybe I should be talking to another because I do it on a regular basis. But all that is, is fear.

Some of us are afraid, so afraid of

abandonment that we won't take care of ourselves and then we won't be attractive. When we're not attractive nobody will approach us, and when nobody approaches us, guess what? We won't have to be abandoned, "Yay!" I'm very serious. We have figured out all kinds of strategies, amazing strategies. "I will not be abandoned. I promise you I will never be abandoned because I will never go out. If I never go out and never meet anybody then guess what?"

People sit with me and say, "I want an intimate relationship."

"What are you willing to do?"

"I'm not willing to do anything. I'm waiting for somebody to come to my house, and when they come, I want them in a certain size, and a certain way. I have a checklist."

Anybody ever notice that? You ever heard people say, "I've got a checklist of who I'm going to be with next time." I'm sitting there thinking, "What? You're going to be in that much control? How many checks can you have, and how many checks can you go without?" It's all based on fear. False Evidence Appearing Real.

I believe that we all yearn for a mutually empowering intimate relationship with someone. You yearn for it. It's in your heart and it is innate. It's what you came here to do. You came to the planet, you were born here spiritually, karma, whatever you want to believe, for the purpose of being in your power, moving towards love, and being connected in mutually empowering intimate relationships. You didn't come here to be less than, and you didn't come here to control others. You came here to share it, to be interconnected and intraconnected. And it's your right, while you're here in this moment, to commit to it. The only thing that will stop you is you, your trauma whisper. It is not because you don't have the skills. It is not because you grew up in a family where everybody was crazy, or alcoholic, or nuts. That's not the reason. Those things developed fear in your body, so now you think, "Well that's the reason."

James Hillman wrote a wonderful

book where he asked, "A hundred years of therapy, are we any better off." His answer was "No". Why? Because we spend more time thinking about and analyzing and figuring out what it is that went wrong in our lives and while we're doing that, guess what we're not doing? We're not living it. You see, you've got something that's natural, which is an emotion called fear. It was given to you, and however the puzzle was put together, it's up to you to figure out. It was given to you so you would be safe. That was it; that's the healthy part of fear. But there's a second part of fear, and this is where the problems come from.

There is a toxic part of fear. It's a fear based on the idea that I'm going to get wounded and I had better be on the lookout. Having nothing to do with your story, having to do with the cultural story that says, "Be on the lookout because bad things happen." You have a constant barrage of people, on a regular basis, saying, "Be afraid. Be afraid. Be afraid. What you should do is be afraid." So, make sure that if you reach out to somebody, or say hello to somebody, don't give them a bad idea about you. I can't say "Hi" to the nice person that stands in the grocery line with me because what if they think I'm coming on to them? So, we stop being nice. Literally, has anyone stood in a line in a grocery store? Next time you stand in a line, see if you don't see how many people, five people standing in a line, nobody saying a word to each other. Don't say anything because if I say something and I happen to be attractive and a nice person and I start being nice, they'll think bad things of me. What the hell are they going to think of you? You're a nice person? Is that awful? "Well, they might think I want to take them home." What do we have these ideas for? Where do they come from?

The second fear, remember the first one is abandonment, these are all a part of our toxic fear. Your second really wonderful fear, that lives in your body and has all stories attached to it, is the fear of loss of power, or engulfment. Most of us don't even see that one. It's like a silent fear. Have you ever been with someone and you realize they're intense and they might take away your power and so you start getting afraid that they are going to make decisions for you? This is called engulfment. We witness someone wanting to get close so we start going, "No, no, no!" Then, have you ever noticed that the ones who don't want to get close to us, we run toward? It's a pursuer/distancer dynamic. There's fear in action. It's amazing to watch how many people come in and sit down in the practice, look at me right square in the eye and say, "I just want you to know, I would really be in love and really be in an intimate relationship if my partner would." I thought, "Well that's convenient. How did you pick that one?"

"Well, I picked that one because the other ones really loved me." You can almost hear people say that as long as someone is running away, I feel comfortable. If they are running towards me, I'll run away. It's amazing to watch the fear, and people will engage relationships like this for years. This huge disconnection. And do you know what that disconnection's name is? Fear. Even though we all say, "I want intimacy."

We say it. We say it to each other. "I want to be in love." We write stories about being in love. We believe in it. We talk about it. At the same time, what we don't talk about is fear. It lives right with love, and do you know what? The hardest thing to know is that to love somebody, to really be intimate with somebody, is to be terrified of that love for them at the same time. It's the duality, and it's finding the middle path. That's the hard thing to recognize because we only want one side. We only want the one side, that one side being. "Yeah, this feels good." That's what we want. We don't understand that life is about having both at the same time. You cannot love, really love somebody unless you feel terrified of losing them, or terrified that they have the ability to take away your power. You can't do it.

Fear is so powerful that it just becomes something like a fog. It comes into relationships, and it hangs out, and it takes over the air. It makes the situation different, and then people get into their patterns with it. "Let's not get close. Let's not make love. Let's not have sex." All of that, believe it or not, is based on fear.

Let me just tell you a great story about couples, because I love listening to their stories. They dance with fear all the time. That's what relationships are about, friendships are about, it's about fear. Your family relationships are about fear. For any of you who are parents, your relationship with your kids is about love and fear, it's about connection and power, you can feel the energy. I was sitting with a couple who were separating after twenty years of being together. They were separating, and they were trying to do it carefully and honestly and up front. At the same time, the reason they were separating is because they hadn't been able to really be affectionate to each other. They hadn't been able to be close. The amazing thing that happened to them was the minute they made the decision, they were close. The fear of engulfment had kept them at a distance from each other, in individual lives, for years. They had stopped making love eleven years prior. Fear is so great, it's in the air, it's in your body. It's amazing. They were as close as they could be in separation, because for the first time, they could look at each other and say, "I don't feel trapped." The whole time they had been fighting against the fear of feeling trapped. It took over the airwaves. Love had gotten lost and fear had taken over. It had come in like the fog and it had taken over. It happens with one person after another.

The third fear is the fear of toxic shame; the awful, yucky feeling that we are supposed to be silent about. Even when we expose our grief, our sadness, our despair, our helplessness, we'll talk about grief, and anger, and sadness, and fear, and bargaining, and re-establishment; but we won't talk about toxic shame, our historical residue. How many of you have felt toxic shame? When you have been hurt and criticized in your life, you have this awful feeling that something about you is wrong. As this wonderful woman said to me, "I just want you to know that in my core, I'm damaged. I feel so ashamed of who I am that I'm not sure that I could even be lovable." And so you can hear her struggle; on one hand, "I want a relationship," on the other hand, "I'm not sure I'm lovable." The voice of toxic shame.

What you do, is you make sure you don't enter into a relationship unless you've got guarantees that this one will work out right and perfectly, so that way I will never feel toxic shame again. You want to make sure that this is The One. So, you hold back. We hold back our affection. We come up with rules like, "You've got to know the person for twelve weeks before you kiss them." Or you come up with other rules like, "Don't say 'I love you' for three months." Or some kind of foolish thing to try to test that you're okay. Or how about the rule that, "If you've been in a relationship and you've got out of one, you've got to grieve for a certain period of time before you get in another one." What are all these rules? Authority issues are really about that fear of engulfment, the feeling of loss of power and control.

It is hard. It is incredibly hard to be in power and control and to be connected at the same time. It is, without question, your right, not a need, not a want, it's your right, it is in your soul to have both. That's what you came to do; to be a powerful human being and to be connected. You see, a culture that says, "Be the individual, be powerful, be strong" minimizes the relational. Cultures that are highly relational, minimize the individual. Neither one is correct.

It is about being a powerful woman, and being connected. It is not your vision as a woman to just be connected. It's not your story that to be in relationship makes you somebody. The story is that you're powerful and you're in a relationship. And for men, the story has been written, clearly, that what you have got to do is be powerful, be in yourself, achieve, do well.

That's only half of the equation. When

you've got one half that's wanting connection, and the other is thinking that their story is about power, they need to be integrated, and now you can see the fear. You can almost feel the palpability of that fear that is so, so powerful.

If you take men and the socialization of boys and men, and it goes all the way through the lineage of years and years of constant messages of, "Be strong, be tough, be a man, show little emotion." And if you do show any emotion, don't make it fear, or sadness, or shame; make it anger. We'll give you that one emotion. Any other feelings have to translate through the funnel. In other words, if you've got some fear, if you've got hurts, if you've got toxic shame, then we've got to funnel it through, and it's got to drop out the funnel as anger.

Now, what we'll do is bring women along, and what we'll do is make them terrified of their anger. We will just take away all of their anger. Hey, if you want to make sure a whole class of people, a whole group of people never gets powerful, take away their anger. If you want to make somebody unempowered, take away their anger. Anger is a catalyst for change. The only way you can change your life is to get frustrated, get irritated, sort of say, "No! Enough!" To take away your power, what I'll do is just make sure that you stay stable and okay with your life, I'll shame you. If you ever get mad as a woman, I'll just call you a name, the "b" word, "bitch" If by any chance, you're a man who's got feelings and the only one you can have is anger, then you rush, with all of your feelings toward her who's going, "No! No anger! I am afraid of your anger." And he's saying, "I'm afraid of your nurturance. I'm afraid of your sadness. I'm afraid of your warmth. I can't do those things." So now you get these two people terrified even to have a conflictual conversation, a difficult emotional conversation.

I could be totally wrong, but the more I listen to people, the more I realize that most of the time in their relationships, they survive, they do alright. But five to ten percent get frustrated with each other because their history has been triggered. One of those three fears: abandonment, engulfment, or toxic shame has been triggered. And once they get hooked and they try having this conversation, the dance starts. "You are..." "No, you are..." And it goes back and forth, and the energy goes up and it becomes ever more irrational. The mind creates a shift, a position It drops all logic, and things that these people have said to each other and have been saving up for twenty years, or it's one old hurt, the trauma whisper, that they keep using, over and over. They're afraid, they're afraid to relax into each other's arms. They're terrified because of the false evidence that this person will either abandon me, will take away my power, or will shame me, and I will do whatever I have to do to make sure that that doesn't happen. I will scan your conversations. I'll watch your words, and I will watch your actions even more closely which speak much louder than your words.

I sat with this wonderful sixteen-year-old boy who watched his father, who had a substance use issue. He watched his father start drinking again. As he watched his father, he counted. He told me exactly how much alcohol was in the bottle. He shared with me, as he watched as witness, with a scanner on his head because of his fear. He was watching how far the bottle would go down in a given day. He would look at me and say, "Do you know he drank that much today?" He saw the six-pack cartons in the trash, knowing that his dad hid the beer in the vegetable bin.

You see that's what fear does to you. You start scanning everything, and you find the evidence. I guarantee that if you use your fear to scan, you will find the evidence. The next relationship, if you choose to be in one, you'll find how that person will disappoint you. I guarantee it. You will find the fear, because the truth is, it's your fear. It's going to keep coming up until you realize the lesson in the story of Michael, which is that you have to talk about it. The reason that we yearn, the reason that we are brought together, the reason that we even have a yearning to be together, the reason that we want mutually empowering intimate relationships in our lives, and we want to love, and we want to love our children, the reason that we want to do that is to heal the hurts.

I'm a scuba diver. Watching sharks, there's a little tiny fish on the shark that cleans it. They're in a loving relationship. The fish cleans the shark. The skin of the shark can feel what is going on around it and the shark never hurts this little tiny fish. Do you know why? They're in a mutually agreed upon relationship. That little tiny fish cleans the fins, the little parts of the gills of the shark, it even goes right up against the mouth, and the shark never bites, because it understands.

If I'd want anything for you, it is for you to understand that loving relationships are the only way that you can heal your fears. You can't do it in your head. I'm sorry. You can't do it by yourself. I'm sorry. You see, that's why there's a yearning to be in relationships. Because once it comes in it all comes up. Not at first because it wants to get this little relationship going, it's called romance. "Ooh yes!" A little smooching, kind of nice, feels good. And then it feels like shit breaks loose. All of the sudden the chaos starts and the little fear stuff comes up. Fear starts to come, and if you watch it, it's really an amazing thing. When people have been hurt in an accident, they do well right away. But what they don't realize is twenty days later, the whole thing starts to vibrate in their bodies. That's what happens to us. It doesn't happen right away, when you first meet somebody. It often happens as time goes on, the scanner, the fear comes up.

What I'm asking you to do, and it doesn't really matter to me if you choose a lover, a partner, but what I am going to ask you to do is don't isolate yourself out of fear. Allow yourself to invite more people into your life. Reach out and get more people. It won't all work. Some people will abandon you. Some people will be critical. But it's like gold mining. Take that life of yours and put it into the river, shake it up, pull out the big stuff, and you'll get a nugget. I promise you, you will never get a nugget unless you put the pan in the water, and unless you go for it on some level. And when the little fear comes in your head and starts to talk to you, "Be careful here, you better be careful. You know that this won't work out for you anyways, right?" All of those voices.

That's when I'm going to ask you to dance with fear. Our fear, right then, was there to protect you. And you can say, *Old Fear. Thank you for protecting me, but I'm going to make a different decision. I'm going to go for love, for friendship, for connection; to my son, to my children, to my family, to my friends, to my lover, to my partner, whatever. You see, old friend, old friend, you're false evidence now. I don't need you anymore. You can come and dance with me, because I know you ain't going away, you're going to stay here all of the way to the end, to the last breath that I take on this time. But you see I'm here to make friends with you, but not to let you be in charge of my life.*

You see, I want you to dance with fear. I want you to understand that it's there. No more denial of it. If I can get you to do anything, get that little microscope inside and say, "Where oh where is my fear? I know you're hiding. Come out." And if you want to know how to get it to come out, just lean towards somebody and see if you don't feel it.

And if you don't feel it yet, just lean a little closer.

ABOUT THE AUTHOR

Stephen R. Andrew LCSW, LADC, CCS is a storyteller, consultant, community organizer and trainer who maintains a compassion-focused private practice and facilitates weekly men's, coed, women's, and Motivational Interviewing learning groups. He provides coaching and training domestically and internationally for social service agencies, health care providers, substance abuse counselors, criminal justice, and other groups on motivational interviewing, supervision, ethics for caring services professionals, men's work, and the power of group work. Stephen lives in Portland, Maine with his sweet wife Hilary, and is the proud father of Sebastian.

Making it happen is our commitment to the world ~50% of our profits will go to the (not- for- profit), AGAPE Inc., dedicated to providing support services and education to create compassionate solutions that strengthen our communities.

www.dignitymaine.com

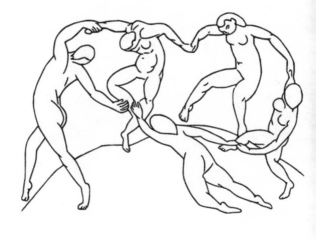